I AM CONFIDENT

MISS MOLLY'S
SCHOOL OF CONFIDENCE

Zanna Davidson

Illustrated by Rosie Reeve

Nice to meet you. Please, come and join us.

Designed by Tabitha Blore
Edited by Anna Milbourne

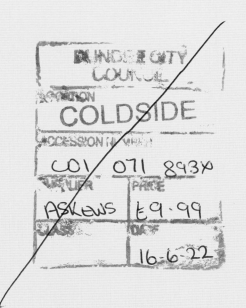

Meet Rosie Rabbit.
She is shy, and scared of many things.

Rosie doesn't like playing outside.

Or going to new places.

Or trying new activities.

And Rosie *really* doesn't like walking through the forest.

It's so dark and scary!

It's okay, Rosie. We can go around the lake instead.

5

On their way around the lake,
the Rabbit family met old Mrs. Robinson.
"Good morning," she said, smiling.
Everyone smiled back, except for Rosie,
who was looking down at the ground.

"Do you worry about a lot of things, Rosie?" asked Mrs. Robinson.
Rosie nodded. "I do," she said, quietly.
"Then I know the place for you! Miss Molly's School of Confidence.
It's just around the corner. My grandson went there, and he loved it."

And as they rounded the corner, there it was…

"We think Rosie might need your help," said Mama Rabbit.
Miss Molly smiled at Rosie. "Will you come and join us today?"
she said. "Don't worry, your parents will pick you up later."
"Okay," whispered Rosie, and she followed Miss Molly inside.

9

Rosie's first lesson was with Mr. Moose, in the BEING POSITIVE CLASS. "Let's begin by feeling good about ourselves," said Mr. Moose. "And one of the best ways to do that is to get moving. Let's reach for the stars!"

"Next we're going to try getting rid of thoughts that make us feel bad. I want each of you to write one down on a piece of paper."

"Congratulations, class! You've all made an EXCELLENT start!"

"Next time you find yourself having a thought that makes you feel bad, I want you to picture yourself scrumpling it up and throwing it away!"

"Did you know," Mr. Moose went on, "it really helps to say encouraging things to yourself as much as you can? Can you each think of something good that you can say about yourself, or something that you're proud of?"

I am kind!

I am brave!

I deserve kindness.

I never give up.

I'm important to my friends.

I believe in ME!

I'm loved by my family.

I am enough.

I am strong and I am smart!

I make good unicorn noises!

I know lots about dinosaurs.

I like being green.

I can't think of anything.

How about coming here today? That's brave!

"Excellent work, class," said Mr. Moose. "Now, I'd like you all to get into pairs and say something that you're worried or feeling bad about. Then see if your partner can work out how to turn your negative feeling into something positive."

"You've all done so well," said Mr. Moose, "you're ready for your next lesson. It's time to TRY NEW THINGS with Mrs. Owl."

Mrs. Owl was very excited to welcome everyone to her classroom.

I'd like you all to start learning a new skill today. What would you like to try?

- CLIMB A TREE
- GO ON A BOAT
- RIDE A BIKE OR SKATEBOARD
- DO A CARTWHEEL
- DO A JIGSAW PUZZLE
- BUILD A TOWER

I want to make friends with Rosie... but what if she doesn't want to be friends with me?

I want to learn to ride a bike!

I've always thought going out in a boat would be nice... But what if I'm no good at it?

I'll learn to do a cartwheel.

13

"It doesn't matter if you make mistakes or get things wrong," Mrs. Owl told the class. "In fact, it's almost impossible to learn without making mistakes."

But Rosie Rabbit still wasn't sure about going out in a boat.
"The water looks so scary…" she said.
"Take it one step, or hop, at a time," suggested Mrs. Owl.
"If something seems too difficult, it helps to set yourself some little goals along the way. Ms. Pelican will help you."

"When you feel comfortable," said Ms. Pelican,
"just splash your feet in the water."
Rosie Rabbit took a deep breath.

Once Rosie felt ready, she climbed into the boat.

Rosie began to row the boat away from the shore, and then...

BUMP! The boat crashed into the dock. "Oh no!" cried Rosie, as a wave SPLASHED over the side. Then Rosie dropped her oar, which PLOPPED into the water.

I've messed up!

No, you haven't. Look how far we've come. You've got this, Rosie.

And I've caught your oar!

SPLASHHHHH

"You see," said Ms. Pelican, when they got back to shore. "You don't have to be perfect. You were brave enough to go out in the boat, and that's an excellent first step."

It WAS fun – maybe next time I'll go all the way across the lake!

I think you've done wonderfully today.

Back in the classroom, Mrs. Owl looked proudly at her students. "You all rose to the challenge of trying something new," she said. "And many of you have learned that it helps to set yourself little goals along the way."

"Would anyone else like to set themselves some new goals?" asked Mrs. Owl.

Goals help you to see how you're progressing. And things seem less scary if you break them into small steps.

I want to get really good at gnawing! I'll start with small twigs... and work up to whole trees!

I'm going to try hiding nuts and not forgetting where they are, so I'll have lots of nuts to eat in winter!

I'm going to try talking to someone I don't know at school.

Me too. It might help me come out of my shell.

"When you're at home," said Mrs. Owl, "I want you to imagine youself achieving your goal. Believing in it will help make it happen!"

After lunch, Mrs. Owl took everyone to the FEELING GRATEFUL classroom, where their next teacher, Professor Porcupine, was waiting for them. "Greetings!" she said. "I'd like us all to think about the things we feel grateful, or lucky, about. Thinking about these things can help us feel good about ourselves... and boost our confidence!"

"What about you, Professor?" asked Archie Armadillo.

"And did you know," Professor Porcupine went on, "you all have something else to be grateful for – your own special talent! Everyone has something they're good at. It can be something you love doing, or part of your personality. Can you think what yours might be?"

Mine is climbing trees!

I don't think I've got a special skill.

Yes, you do! You're an amazing friend! I never could have gone in that boat without your help.

I'm a good listener.

I'm really good at eating honey.

I have nimble paws. I can open anything!

I'm great at POUNCING!

My mama says I have a lovely smile.

You do, Betty Beaver.

Then everyone looked up, as they heard someone clapping. Miss Molly was standing in the doorway, smiling. "I'm so proud of everyone," she said. "You've all come so far today. Would you like to join me for your last lesson? It's all about being calm. I thought we could have it by the lake."

One of the best places for being calm is outside.

But what does being calm have to do with confidence?

"Being calm helps you to let go of all the things that are worrying you," said Miss Molly. "To feel calm, try doing just one simple thing, like watching a blade of grass."

Or you could look up at the branches of a tree waving in the wind, or an insect crawling along a leaf.

"Try concentrating on what you're looking at, and nothing else," said Miss Molly. "Let's see if we can all quietly watch the world for a few minutes."

"How did that make you feel?" asked Miss Molly.

"If you want to feel calm, but can't go outside, there are breathing exercises you can do too," said Miss Molly.

"Or you can make yourself feel calm by lying down.
Imagine yourself in a lovely place – like floating
on a cloud, or being by a warm, crackling fire.
Squeeze your body, so your muscles feel all tight.
Then slowly relax each part of your body,
from your toes to the top of your head.
You can start by wiggling your toes!"

When everyone was feeling calm and relaxed, Miss Molly told them about their last activity for the day. "We're all going to grow our own dreams! I'm giving each of you a little pot with a label on it. I want you to write down a hope or a dream that you have. Then plant a seed in the pot."

Cover your seed with earth and sprinkle it with water.

"You can take your seed home and watch it grow. It will need water and a warm, sunny spot. And remember," Miss Molly went on, "as you look after your seedlings, try to give the same care to your hopes and dreams."

When all the seeds had been planted, Miss Molly turned to the class. "Let's think about the challenges you faced today and how you overcame them."

I came out of my shell!

I went on a boat on the lake even though I'm scared of water.

I spoke to new friends even though I felt shy.

I've set goals for myself.

I threw away my worried feeling and didn't think about it all day.

I taught my first class!

Well done, Mr. Moose!

I learned about gratitude. Thank you for teaching us!

I stayed still for a whole minute!

"Next time you're not feeling confident," said Miss Molly, "remember a moment when you felt positive and what you were doing and thinking. It will help you to feel that way again."

"Now, before you go home," said Miss Molly, "let's look at this poster and remind ourselves of all the helpful tips we've learned."

I have a little poster for you to take home, too. You could try making your own positivity display!

Be **grateful** - write lists of all the good things in your life.

Say encouraging things to yourself.

Remember - you **don't** have to be perfect.

HOW TO BOOS

Throw away negative thoughts!

Spend time **outside** each day.

YOUR **CONFIDENCE!**

Try turning negative thoughts into **POSITIVE** ones.

Get **moving!**

Do breathing exercises to **keep calm.**

Find your **talent!**

challenge yourself to try new things.

Set small **goals** for yourself.

Don't worry about making mistakes. You can't learn without them!

Look after your **hopes** and **dreams.**

1 2 3

Last of all, Miss Molly gave everyone a badge to wear.

"You've all done wonderfully at my School of Confidence," she said.
"Congratulations!"

Soon the grown-ups arrived to take everyone home.
Rosie couldn't wait to tell her parents about her day.

Goodbye and good luck! You're always welcome here.

I feel much more confident now! I even WENT IN A BOAT!

Wow! That's wonderful, Rosie. It sounds like you tried really hard today.

Then the Rabbit family all walked home together.

"We won't go through the forest," said Mama Rabbit. "I know it's too scary for you." "It's okay," said Rosie. She looked down at her badge and smiled. "I can do this!" she said, bravely. "It will be an adventure!"

Oh, but the thing is... I'm scared of the forest too.

Meadow   Forest

Rosie reached for her father's paw. "Don't worry, Papa," she said. "Take a deep breath and we'll just take it one hop at a time. Are you ready?"

I'm ready.

That night, Papa Rabbit tucked Rosie up in bed.
"Thank you," he said. "You even helped *me* feel more
confident. I'm so proud of you."

Rosie Rabbit smiled. "Actually," she said,
"I'm a little bit proud of me too!"

Design Manager: Nicola Butler

Digital manipulation: Nick Wakeford and John Russell